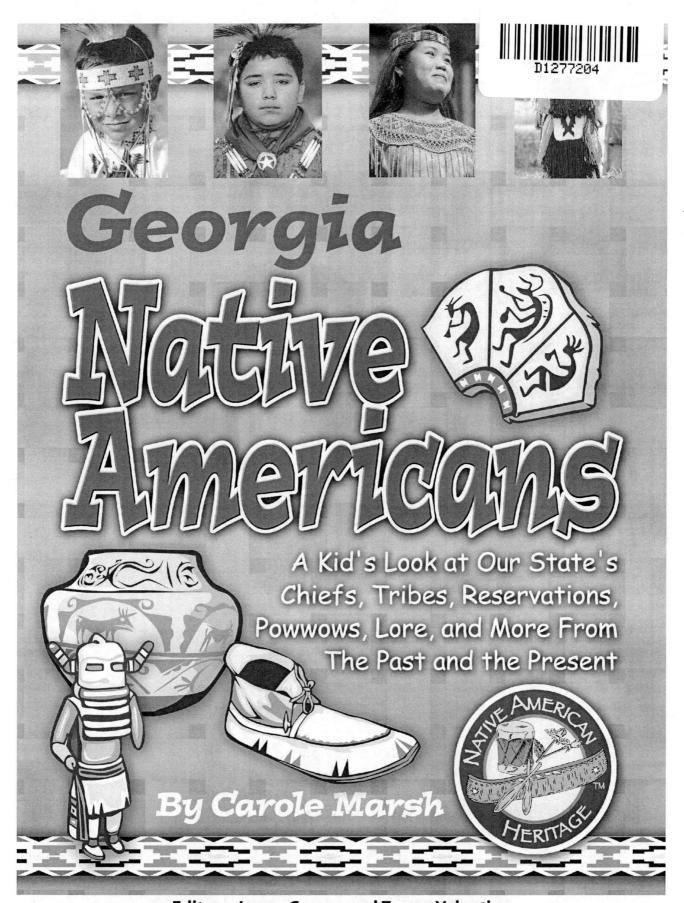

Georgia Native Americans

A Kid's Look at Our State's Chiefs, Tribes, Reservations, Powwows, Lore, and More From The Past and the Present

By Carole Marsh

Editors: Jenny Corsey and Teresa Valentine
Graphic Design: Lynette Rowe • Cover Design: Victoria DeJoy

1

Published by

GALLOPADE™
INTERNATIONAL

800-536-2GET
www.gallopade.com

Gallopade is proud to be a member of these educational organizations and associations:

The National School Supply and Equipment Association (NSSEA)
American Booksellers Association (ABA)
Virginia Educational Media Association (VEMA)
Association of Partners for Public Lands (APPL)
Museum Store Association (MSA)
National Association for Gifted Children (NAGC)
Publishers Marketing Association (PMA)
International Reading Association (IRA)
Association of African American Museums (AAAM)

Native American Heritage™ Series

Native American
Big Activity Book

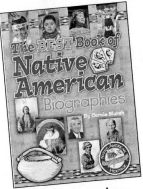

Native American
Biographies

Native American
Coloring Book

Native American
Heritage Book

Native American
Timeline

Georgia STATE STUFF™

My First Pocket Guide: Georgia

My First Book About Georgia

Georgia Coloring Book

The Big Georgia Reproducible Activity Book

Jeopardy: Answers & Questions About Our State

Georgia "Jography!": A Fun Run Through Our State

Georgia Gamebooks

Georgia Bingo Games

Georgia Illustrated Timelines

Georgia Project Books

Georgia Bulletin Board Set

Georgia PosterMap

Georgia Stickers

Let's Discover Georgia! CD-ROM

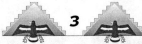

3

Word from the Author

Hello!

I hope you are as interested in North America's wonderful Indian heritage as I am!

Like most kids, I grew up thinking of Indians as the other half of Cowboys. Today, of course, we are getting a much clearer & more accurate picture of what the first peoples on our land were all about. These "facts" are much more fascinating than anything Hollywood can make up. And you probably won't find much of this information in your history textbook!

I am 1/16 Cherokee. This is something I am very proud of & happy about. My grandmother was 1/4 Cherokee. She had tan skin, long gray hair & a very Indian look – especially if I did something bad! Her maiden name was Carrie Corn. Of course, when she got married, she took her husband's name, so it was many years before I learned to appreciate the significance of my native heritage.

Today, I'm trying to make up for lost time by exploring my roots as deeply as I can. One of the most interesting things I've learned is how fascinating all of the Indian tribes are – in the past, the present & future!

As you read about "your" Indians, remember that all native peoples were part of an ever-changing network of time, ideas, power & luck — good & bad. This is certainly a history that is not "dead," but continues to change – often right outside our own back doors! – all the time.

Carole Marsh
She-Who-Writes

PS: Many references show different spellings for the same word. I have tried to select the most common spelling for the time period described. I would not want to be in an Indian spelling bee!

A is for . . .

Autumn Green Corn

The annual Cherokee harvest festival.

Apalachee

A Georgia river and town take their name from the early Florida tribe, now extinct.

Altar

A platform made of rocks or animal skulls; some had bowls, feathers, rattles, or skins on them. Indians prayed at these altars for things like good crops or expert hunting skills.

Aborigine

A member of the earliest known population of a region.

Awl

An Indian's "needle." Often made from wood, thorns, bone, or metal, it was used to punch holes in skins so they could be sewn together.

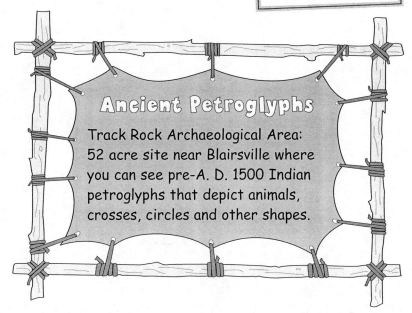

Ancient Petroglyphs

Track Rock Archaeological Area: 52 acre site near Blairsville where you can see pre-A. D. 1500 Indian petroglyphs that depict animals, crosses, circles and other shapes.

Arrow

A long, slender shaft made of reed, cane, or wood; pointed tip was attached to one end and split feathers to the other. Feathers helped the arrows fly straight.

Arrowhead

The pointed tip of an arrow, made of bone, antler, wood, or iron. Some tips had barbs that would embed themselves in flesh. These barbs made it difficult for an enemy to remove the arrowhead from a wound.

Adze

An Indian woodworking tool used to cut, scrape, or gouge; often used to hollow dugout canoes. Blades were made of stone, shell, bone or copper.

Adobe

Brick made of mud plus straw and dried in the sun. Houses made of adobe are cool inside, even in high temperatures, because the walls are so thick.

 **is for . . .**

Blowgun

The Cherokee used this weapon that we usually associate with the Pygmy of Africa. The darts were made of thin splints of wood or reed. The end was wrapped in cotton or thistle down.

Ball Ground

A town said to have gotten its name because the Cherokee and Creek played a mock battle ball game here to decide how hunting lands should be divided. (The Cherokee won!)

Band

A subdivision of an Indian tribe. In earlier times, a band was sometimes created when part of a tribe split off from the main group. The band also chose new leadership.

Baskets

Some were woven and others were coiled. Baskets were made from roots, grasses, barks, and other natural materials.

Bosomworth, Mary

Creek Indian woman and interpreter for Governor Oglethorpe; also known as Mary Musgrove and Mary Matthews (probably because of her name changes with her 3 marriages to different white men.)

Bissasha

Choctaw town in Newton County; name means "the blackberries are ripe there."

Bow

Made from wood, horn or bone. Georgia Indian children learned how to use bows. The bowstring was made from animal gut, rawhide or twisted vegetable fibers.

Bone

Animal bones were used by Georgia Indians to make buttons, whistles and other items.

Beads

Made of wood, shells, claws, minerals, seeds — you name it! Worn by Indians and traded with settlers for glass beads.

C is for . . .

Clan
A tribal unit. Members are descended from the same ancestor.

Chief
Leader of a tribe. Different titles meant different things. Some members were made chief because they owned deeds to land. Chieftainship was often inherited, usually from the mother!

Contact Period
What historians call the era in the 1500s when Native Americans first met Europeans. This meeting changed the lifestyle of the Georgia Indians more than anyone could ever have anticipated!

Chattanooga
A Cherokee word that means "crow's nest"; also the name of a creek in Georgia.

Cherokee
One of the most famous southeastern tribes, they once roamed the mountains of Virginia, West Virginia, Tennessee, North Carolina, South Carolina, Georgia, and Alabama. The Cherokee sided with the English during the Revolutionary War, but did not participate in the battles. In 1827, they adopted a governmental system based on that of the United States called the "Cherokee Nation." For many years, the Cherokee lived in peace and shared respect with white settlers. When gold was discovered in their Georgia territory, the Cherokee were forced to leave their lands and move west. This tragic march was called the Trail of Tears.

Confederacy
A union of different groups of people. A confederacy in Indian culture was a group of tribes that agreed not to fight with each other. They agreed to live peacefully. Sometimes the tribes shared culture and language.

Choctaw
A tribe of excellent farmers and traders. It is believed that the Choctaw and the Chickasaw came to the South as one people and then separated. The United States used the Choctaw language as a special code during World Wars I and II.

"Cave People"
What the Cherokee were sometimes called because of their hillside dwellings.

Chekilli
Main chief of the Creek confederacy when Georgia was settled in 1733; he visited England 2 years later.

Creek
A widespread and powerful nation of the Southeast. The Lower Creek lived mostly in Georgia. They built their villages along wooded rivers, creeks, and streams. The Creek were skilled farmers. Villages were organized into "red towns" for warriors or "white towns" for peacemakers.

7

 **D is for . . .**

 Dance

There were Indian dances for every occasion: war, peace, hunting, rain, good harvests, etc. Drums, rattles, and flutes of bone or reed provided the music. Dancers often chanted or sang while performing. Steps were not easy to learn and required consistent practice.

Descendants

The first Georgia Indians were descendants of primitive hunters who crossed the Bering Strait from Asia to what is now Alaska. At that time, glacial ice still covered most of North America. These people were the true discoverers of the "New World!"

Disease

Georgia Indians had no immunity to the diseases that white explorers, colonists and settlers brought to their lands. These diseases included smallpox, measles, tuberculosis and others, which ravaged the tribes in great epidemics that killed many, and sometimes all, members of a tribe.

Dahlonega

Dahlo means "yellow metal" in the Cherokee language. The Indians knew that this odd ore could be found in Georgia's northern creeks long before the whites "discovered" gold there and threw the Indians off their native lands.

Devil Town

Also known as Skeinah, a former Cherokee settlement in Fannin County.

Dishes

Made from clay, bark, wood, stone, and other materials, depending on what was available and what food they would be used for.

Distinctive Fishing

Some Georgia Indians fished in a different way. When water levels ran low, they would add special ground-up plants to the water that made fish rise to the surface, belly up!

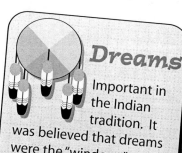 **Dreams**

Important in the Indian tradition. It was believed that dreams were the "windows" to the soul. Many thought a person's hidden desires were expressed in dreams.

8

 **is for . . .**

Eagle

An animal used in many Indian ceremonies. Eagle feathers attached to war bonnets and shields communicated an Indian's rank in his tribe and what kinds of deeds he had done. Feathers also adorned rattles, pipes, baskets, and prayer sticks.

Emperor Brim

Creek chief who organized war parties in 1715 to drive out English colonists trying to enter the state from South Carolina. The Indians carried out a bloody massacre against English settlements. But when the Indians got near Charles Town, the English finally drove the Indians back into Georgia's wilderness!

Emistesigo

Chief of the Upper Creeks; was more than 6 feet tall! Fought the British. Attacked a large force of soldiers and took their cannon away in hand-to-hand combat. He and 17 fellow warriors died. He was only 30 years old.

Etowah Indian Mounds

Near Cartersville. This National Historic Landmark is a large Indian site with 7 mounds surrounded by a partially filled moat. Materials recovered from excavations are on display. The Etowah Indians occupied the valley between A. D. 700 and 1650. Several thousand Indians lived in this fortified town.

Echota

Means "unknown"; was the name of several Cherokee villages.

Earrings

Medicine men sometimes pierced male and female ears at special ceremonies. Earrings, which cost parents or relatives a significant amount, symbolized wealth and distinction. The more earrings that an Indian wore, the greater his honor. Some earrings measured 12 inches in length!

English

In the 1800s, the U.S. government built boarding schools for Indian children throughout the nation. Children were forced to leave their homes and families to live at these schools. They were required to learn English and not speak their native languages.

Epidemics

Few Indians possessed immunity to the deadly diseases, like smallpox and measles, which European explorers and settlers brought to the New World. As a result, great population loss took place. Sometimes entire tribes became extinct. Epidemics sparked by Hernando De Soto's expedition are estimated to have killed 75% of the native population in the New World.

9

F is for . . .

Fetish

These small objects were thought to hold the spirit of an animal or a part of nature. A fetish could be an object found in nature, such as bone or wood, or it could be a carved object. The fetish was usually small enough to be carried in a small bag or on a cord. The making and use of a fetish was kept secret by its owner and only shared with the one who inherited it.

Fusihatchi

Upper Creek town on the Tallapoosa River in Macon County.

Fightingtown

A Cherokee village located on Fightingtown Creek in Fannin County.

Farmers

Many Georgia Indians, ancient and modern, have farming ways! Even pre-contact Indians tilled and irrigated, raising many important crops. Corn, cotton, beans, squash, melons, sunflowers, gourds, pumpkins and tobacco are all native Indian crops!

Five Civilized Tribes

What the Choctaw, Chickasaw, Seminole, Cherokee, and Creek Indian Tribes were called. The name was given because of how far they had progressed into adopting the ideas and customs of whites.

Fire Drill

A device used by Indians to make fires which consisted of a stick and a piece of wood with a tight hole in it. The stick was twirled rapidly in the hole, creating friction that would ignite shredded grass or wood powder placed nearby to start a fire.

Footwear

Georgia Indians wore different footwear depending on their tribe and environment. Moccasins were made mostly of animal skin. Sandals were made of rawhide or plant material.

First On the Land

Who were some of Georgia's earliest Indian tribes? The Cherokee came into the state from the north; the Muskhogean peoples entered the state from the southwest. These early Georgians found a great place to live, with plenty of wild game such as deer, raccoon, otter and birds to hunt and kill for food, clothing and other uses. They also speared fish and captured turtles with nets.

10

G is for . . .

Games

Adults played ball and other games of chance or skill. Indian children spun tops, fought pretend battles, did target-shooting, walked on stilts, played hide and seek, or competed to see who could hold their breath the longest!

Guale

(say Wallie)

An Indian chief who was friendly to early Spanish soldiers in Georgia. At one time, the entire coastal area of Georgia was called the Guale District.

Go To

Did you know there is an annual Indian Festival and PowWow in Georgia? Go to Stone Mountain Park, just east of Atlanta, in early November. See Indians from around the country dance, and see a "living village"!

Gens

Group of related members from different tribes.

Green Corn Dance

A Creek Indian dance performed during the annual harvest ceremonies.

Gorgets

Beautiful ornaments hung around the neck or from ears; their significance, if any, is unknown.

Gold Fever

The Cherokee were the last Indians left in Georgia. They lived in the northwest corner of the state. They had done everything they could to adopt to the white man's "civilized" ways. They organized an independent government, wrote a constitution and established a capital city (New Echota). Even though they lived in peace and prosperity, it was not enough. When gold was discovered near Dahlonega in 1828, miners flooded onto the Cherokee's land. The Cherokee hired lawyers and took their fight all the way to the U. S. Supreme Court, but still lost the battle to keep their beloved homeland and were forced to move to Oklahoma.

Gourds

Hollowed-out shell of a gourd plant's dried fruit which often grew into a specific shape. Indians raised many species of gourds. They were used for spoons, bowls, masks, rattles, and even storage.

H is for . . .

Hatchet

A small, short-handled ax, primarily used as a tool, not as a weapon. When settlers moved in, stone hatchets were replaced with iron ones.

Hair

Indians used hair as a textile. Hair from bison, mountain sheep, elk, moose, deer, dog, rabbit, beaver, or even humans were used to weave cloth, make wigs, or stuff pillows, balls, dolls or drumsticks.

Horn and Hooves

Indians used animal horn to make spoons and dishes. Hooves were made into rattles and bird beaks were used for decoration.

Hado, Milly

Beautiful daughter of a Seminole chief. When her father sentenced a man to die by being burned to death, she fell on her knees to beg for him to be released. She even threatened to throw herself into the flames if the white man was not set free. Her father did let the man go. Later, after Milly was captured by American soldiers, the man volunteered to marry her to save her. But Milly believed he only did that to repay her kindness and not because he loved her, so she refused.

Head Flattening

The significance of this Choctaw custom, flattening the heads of young children, remains unknown. Experts say flat heads might have symbolized beauty or higher social standing. Parents laid their babies in hinged cradle boards to press their skulls or against boards with weighted leather strips.

Hunters

Early Indian peoples were hunters who used wooden spears with stone points to kill many kinds of large mammals that are extinct today, such as mammoths and mastodons!

Horses

Spaniards brought the horse to America. At first, Indians were afraid of the horse or thought it was sacred. Later, Indians "broke" horses gently, often "hypnotizing" them with a blanket. Horses were used for transportation, trade, barter or payment. Some Indians ate horse meat in hopes of gaining the animal's power.

Hanging Maw

Cherokee Indian chief; his name means "his stomach hangs down"!

How Much Land?

When we read that the Indians gave up their homeland, what exactly are we taking about? Well, in 1773, the Creek and Cherokee of Georgia signed a treaty at Augusta giving England 2.1 million acres of land!

I is for . . .

Inevitable Clash?

Georgia's early Indians were very happy with their new land. But newcomers to Georgia, such as the Spanish, were not happy with fertile land and plenty of wild game, or even rivers filled with fish. They wanted gold and believed they would find cities filled with it here!

Ivy Log

A Cherokee settlement on the Ivy Log Creek in north Georgia. This town was still active at the time the Cherokee were "removed" in 1839.

Indian Removal Act of 1830

This federal act gave President Andrew Jackson the power to relocate tribes east of the Mississippi to an "Indian Territory." The forced removal of the southeast Indians later became known as the "Trail of Tears."

Indian Wars

When the Spanish and English first came to Georgia, Indians often sided with one group or the other. The white men would give the Indians weapons to fight with. Later, of course, it would be the white men against the Indians, who would use those weapons against their former allies!

Indian Springs Museum, Flovilla

Traces the history of Indian Springs. Items on display reflect the stages of Indian civilizations. Includes the treaties signed, Chief McIntosh's Assassination and Creek Indian artifacts. Special programs are held on Indian sign language, hunting techniques, pottery and basket-making.

Indian Ladder

Indians made ladders by trimming branches off a tree. Some were left at consistent intervals to provide steps.

Indian Tribes in Georgia

At one time or another, these tribes have lived in the state of Georgia:
Apalachee, Cherokee, Choctaw, Creek, Guales, Hitchiti, Kashita, Shawnee, Timucan, Yamasee, Yuchi.

Indian

In 1493, Christopher Columbus called the native people he met in North America "Indians" because he mistakenly believed he had sailed to India! Today, this term includes the aborigines of North and South America.

Junaluska

Cherokee chief Junaluska fought with General Andrew Jackson against the Creek Indians at the battle of Horseshoe Bend. He and two other warriors braved enemy fire to steal Creek war canoes at night for the Americans. Their mission helped General Jackson, who had been losing, to win the battle. During the fighting, Junaluska also killed a Creek Indian who nearly killed General Jackson. Years later, when General Jackson became U.S. president, he ordered the Cherokee to leave their lands. Junaluska pleaded with him to spare his people the Trail of Tears journey. But President Andrew Jackson told him, "There is nothing I can do for you."

Jesuits

Roman Catholic priests called Jesuits were among the first to meet and live with the North American Indians. Their writings, sent back to Europe, serve as one of today's best references to early Indian life.

Justice?

After their surrender in the Creek War of 1813-14, General Andrew Jackson forced the Creeks to sign a treaty taking away 23 million acres of land as punishment—from both the warring Creeks and the uninvolved Creeks.

Judicial Termination

Modern term to describe current efforts by various U.S. government agencies and officials (especially the judicial system) to legally decrease the sovereignty of independent Indian tribes.

Johnstown

Cherokee settlement in Hall County on the Chattahoochee River.

Jerked Meat

Thin strips of buffalo, elk, deer or other animal meat which is dried on racks in the sun; also called "jerky."

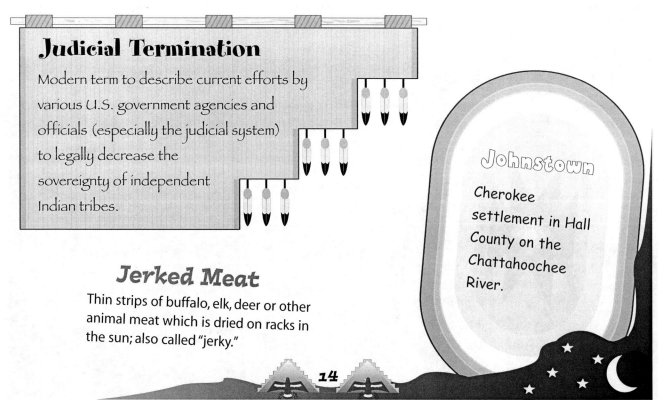

14

 **is for . . .**

Kuhlahi

Former Cherokee settlement in Georgia. Name means "place of the beech tree."

Kolomoki Mounds State Park and Historic Site, Blakely

Historic site of 13th century Indian burial mound and village. Artifacts from excavations are on display.

Killed Pottery

Pottery placed in a grave as an offering to the dead person was called killed pottery. A hole was formed in its base during creation. Often broken pottery was placed in a grave because Indians believed the spirit of the dead person would then be released and could travel.

Knife

Made from various materials such as bone, reed, stone, wood, antler, shell, metal, or animal teeth (bear, beaver, etc.), knives were used as weapons but also creative handiwork.

Kasihta

Creek town on the Chattahoochee River. The Indians here believed they were descended from the Sun.

Knots

Tied on bowstrings, spearhead and arrowhead lashings, snowshoes, and other items, knots were sometimes used to keep track of the days like a calendar—each knot equaled 1 day.

15

 # L is for . . .

Linguistic Families

There are 56 related groups of American Indian languages. A few of these speech families include Iroquoian, Algonquian, Siouan, Muskogean, Athapascan, and Wakashan.

Leggings

Both men and women wore cloth or skin covering, which were often decorated with quills, beads, or painted designs, for their legs.

Lost Tribes of Israel

This historic theory has been floating around since 721 BC. The 10 lost tribes of Israel are supposedly groups of people gathered together by Sargon, the King of Assyria. Some say he cast out 10 of the 12 tribes of Israel. Many have tried to prove that the American Indians are these missing tribes!

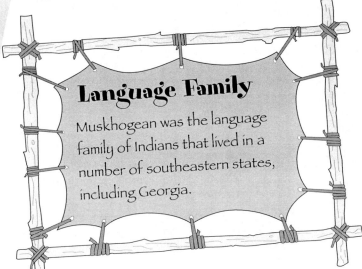

Language Family

Muskhogean was the language family of Indians that lived in a number of southeastern states, including Georgia.

Leatherwood

Cherokee settlement in Franklin County. Possibly named for the chief of the tribe.

Lady of Cofitachiqui

A Muskogee Indian woman who lived on the Savannah River. She was the chieftainess of Cofitachiqui. In 1540, when Spanish explorer Hernando De Soto visited, he was welcomed by the "Lady of Cofitachiqui" who gave him a string of pearls in friendship. De Soto "thanked her" by kidnapping her to be a hostage to protect his party from Indian attacks! After 2 weeks, the Lady escaped. On her way out of the camp, she grabbed a box of pearls that De Soto had previously stolen!

Lance

Spear used for hunting and war. The hunting lance had a short shaft and a broad, heavy head. The war lance was light and had a long shaft.

Long Island

Name of an island in the Tennessee River on the Georgia line. Settled by Cherokee in 1782; destroyed in 1794.

Lariat

These throw ropes made of rawhide, buffalo hair, or horsehair sometimes measured up to 20 feet long!

 is for . . .

McGillivray, Alexander

Chief of the Creek Federation. He kept the southern Indian tribes loyal to England during the Revolutionary War. He also helped make the Indians allies with Spain against settlement in America. In 1790, he signed a peace treaty with George Washington. Later, he broke this treaty and started a new war against the United States.

Maize

Also called Indian Corn. Known as a "cereal" plant because it probably began as some form of grass. The Indians in our state figured out every possible way to use corn as a food. The only thing the white man added was the creation of "corn flakes!"

Moccasins

Indian shoes made of animal skin.

Medicine

Medicine could be good or bad. Medicines or charms were placed in a bag by young warriors and carried at all times. Some of the roots, leaves and bark that Indians in our state used as medicine are being rediscovered and used by today's doctors!

Medicine Man

A person who got the power to heal the sick through a secret means, usually from a dream or visions.

Mound Builders

Georgia is known for the many Indian mounds that can still be seen in our state. Archaeologists think some of the mounds may have been built as early as 8000 B.C. Most of the mounds are made of dirt, although some were made of shells. They were usually built near rivers and streams. Their shape was a flattened pyramid, rings or circles. Some are 60 feet tall! Nearby would have been tribal towns that existed for centuries. Many shards of pottery, arrowheads and even skeletons have been dug up, but we still don't know whether these mounds were used for lookouts, burial grounds or places of worship. What happened to the Mound Builders? It's possible that as early as A.D. 1000 new wandering, warlike tribes began to invade their territories and either defeated them in battle or absorbed them into their own tribes.

17

N is for . . .

New Fire

The Cherokee New Year festival when the perpetual fire in the village was relighted.

Nancy Ward

Said to be the daughter of a British officer and the sister of a chief of the Cherokee Nation. Called "Pretty Woman" by her tribe. Allowed to speak in councils. As a friend to the American colonists, she was able to save many lives, since she could also decide what should be done with captives. Introduced the first cows to the Cherokee and helped them improve their living conditions in many other ways.

Nation

There are many Indian nations that live within the United States, such as the Cherokee Nation. Indian nations are called nations because their governments and laws are independent of and separate from the U.S. government. The federal government must have "government to government" relations with these Indian nations, just as it would with foreign nations, like England or Spain.

Names

Indian names were often changed during one's lifetime. These names could be derived from events that happened during the person's birth, childhood, adolescence, war service, or retirement from active tribal life. Some names came from dreams, some were inherited, and sometimes names were stolen or taken in revenge. Today some Indians maintain old, traditional Indian names, while others take modern names. Since settlers often did not read or write Indian languages, they recorded Indian names phonetically (as they "sounded"). Thus Indian names were often misspelled.

Newspaper

After the Cherokee Nation accepted Sequoya's alphabet in 1821, thousands of Indians learned to read and write in their own language in just a few months! Parts of the Bible were translated into Cherokee. In 1828, the Cherokee Phoenix weekly newspaper was printed in both English and Cherokee. It was the 1st newspaper printed in any North American Indian language.

New Echota Historic Site, Calhoun

1825 capital town of the Cherokee Nation. Museum and 5 historical buildings house archaeological materials used by the Cherokees in the early 1800s. You can research Cherokee genealogy and the Trail of Tears in the library.

Nunna-da-ul-tsun-yi

Cherokee for "the place where they cried"; what the survivors of the forced march to Oklahoma called the path they had traveled. Today we call it the "Trail of Tears."

 **is for . . .**

Ogeechee

Small tribe of Yuchi who lived on the Ogeechee River.

Outpost Replica

A reconstruction of a palisade used to ward off Creek and Seminole attacks; located near Blakely.

Oconee's Fish Trap Cut

Site of 2 Indian ceremonial mounds on the Oconee River. A cut, 100 yards into the bank, was used to trap fish. It was built as early as 1000 B. C.!

Oil

Indians extracted oil from the many layers of fat that came with fresh bear meat. The fat was boiled down in earthen pots to produce the oil, which was stored in gourds and pots. The oil was used for cooking and even beautifying the body! Indians would mix red pigment with the oil, add the fragrances of cinnamon and sassafras, and rub it all over their bodies.

Ocmulgee

Name of a Lower Creek town in Dougherty County.

Orators

Many Indian leaders were excellent public speakers. Powerful and dramatic speakers were vital to leaders who wanted to influence their tribe. Watch for famous Indian quotations in literature and textbooks!

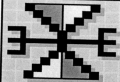

Ocmulgee National Monument, Macon

Site of 7 mounds constructed by a group of farming Indians 1,000 years ago. Around 2,000 people lived here at one time! The museum contains archaeology on the culture of the Indians and the 5 other Indian groups that have lived in this area since. There is also a Creek Indian Trading Post and a library.

19

P is for . . .

Powwow

The original form of the word meant "medicine man." Medicine men would often use noise motion and confusion to scare away harmful spirits and cure people. It was also a gathering to talk about political matters. Today, the powwow is an event where Indians gather to sing, perform ceremonial dances, and share cultural pride and traditions.

Picture This!

Chattahoochee means "picture rocks" or "rock mark," which refers to the picture writing found on the rocks in the area of the upper part of the Chattahoochee River in Georgia where the Lower Creeks had a town.

Prehistoric Indians

Stone tools that date back as far as 10,000 B.C. have been found in Georgia! But we know almost nothing about the early hunters and gatherers who first lived here. The tools and mounds they left behind intrigue us, but provide few answers to our many questions about who were truly the first "Native Americans" in our state.

Pemmican

Indian food made of animal meat, which was dried in the sun, pounded together with fat and berries. The mixture was packed into skin bags and used primarily while on the trail.

Paint

Indians used many natural materials to make paint, like clay mixed with oil or grease. Yellow "paint" was made with the gall bladder of a buffalo! Why did they paint their faces or bodies? Indians used paint to look scary or beautiful, to disguise themselves, or to protect their skin from sunburn or insect bites. Indians often applied red paint because it symbolized strength and success. That is why settlers often referred to the Indians as Red Men.

Papoose

An American Indian infant aged between birth and one year is called a papoose. This word also refers to the way infants were bundled and carried by its mother. A papoose spent most of his or her days snugly wrapped in a kind of cradle made of skins or bark and a wooden frame that hung on the mother's back. This sturdy frame also allowed a mother to lean her papoose against a tree or rock within sight as she worked.

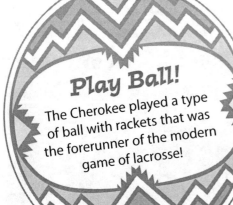

Play Ball!

The Cherokee played a type of ball with rackets that was the forerunner of the modern game of lacrosse!

Pottery

Indian pottery was made from built-up spirals of clay that were molded or paddled, or a combination of the two methods. Most pottery served as cooking vessels.

Q is for . . .

Quillwork

Indians used the quills of porcupine or birds to make a type of embroidery. Quills were dyed with juice from berries and other materials. When they were ready to be used, the quills were either mashed with teeth or softened with hot water and flattened with rocks. The quills were then laced into moccasins, shirts, pipe covers, and other items. Beads which Indians received by trading with settlers eventually replaced quillwork.

Quite Some Quartz!

You can see the amazing Rock Eagle Effigy Mound in Eatonton. Woodland Period Indians are thought to have created this huge mound, which is 102 feet long and 120 feet wide, with a height of 10 feet! It has been called the most perfect effigy mound in the United States. White quartz rocks were piled high about 6,000 years ago to form an effigy of a bird with spread wings. It is thought to have been used for ceremonial purposes. A tower at the site offers an elevated view!

Quiver

Case used to hold arrows; made of woven plant materials or animal skins.

Quirt

A short riding whip with a wood, bone, or horn handle.

Qualla

The Qualla Arts and Crafts Mutual is a cooperative artists' and craftspeople's organization of 300 Eastern Cherokee artists and craftspeople. Established in 1946, and long recognized as the most outstanding Indian owned and operated arts and crafts cooperative in America!

R is for . . .

Rain Dancing

The rain dance ceremony, performed to encourage rainfall, was common among Indian religions because good weather is vital for a successful harvest. Rainmakers were in tune with nature; there are actual reported cases of Indians producing or preventing rain!

Roots

Indians used plant roots for food, medicine, dye, baskets, cloth, rope, salt, flavoring, and just to chew!

Respect

Cherokee Indians were very respected by white peoples. The Cherokee owned farms and sent their children to the white schools. In 1825, records show that 47 white men and 73 white women married into the Cherokee Nation.

Red Chief

One of the 2 chiefs of a Cherokee village. Gave advice concerning warfare and was in charge of lacrosse games. He chose the War Woman. The other chief was the White Chief, also called Most Beloved Man. He helped with making farming decisions, lawmaking, disputes and also played a part in religious ceremonies.

Rawhide

Untanned animal hide. The "green" hide was stretched on the ground or over a frame. Flesh and fat were removed. The skin was dried, washed, then buried with wood ashes which made the hair come off. Used by the Georgia Indian to make drumheads, lash lodge poles, mend broken objects and in many other ways.

Reservations

The U.S. government set aside, or "reserved," land for the Indians. These reservations originally served as a sort of prison during the beginning stages of Indian removal. At that time, reservations provided the government with some control over Indian activity and residency. This land was usually considerably less desirable land than the Indians' native territories. Today's reservations are lands that are tribally held, yet protected by the government.

Ross, Chief John

You can see his 1797 historical house with displays of Indian artifacts and the Cherokee alphabet in Rossville. He was the 1st president of the National Council of Cherokees and was opposed to the U.S. government's goal to take tribal lands. But he was forced to lead his people west across the Mississippi River. He was named Chief of the Cherokee Nation in 1839. For the rest of his life, he fought for the rights of his people.

S is for...

Seminole Wars

Seminole Indians

Formerly lived in southern Georgia and Alabama, migrated to northern Florida in the 1700s, and came together to form the Seminole tribe

Shaman

Medicine man and spiritual leader who was supposed to have special healing power from another world.

In 1812, the Georgia Militia under General Newman invaded Florida and the Seminole, under King Wayne, were defeated. General Andrew Jackson started the First Seminole War in 1817, using the runaway slaves the Seminole hid as an excuse to send in an army. This invasion also started a war with Spain! The Second Seminole War of 1835-42 was the costliest Indian war ever, with army losses of 1,500 men, $30 million dollars, and no victory over the Seminole. The Third Seminole War was from 1855-58. Again the army couldn't contain the Seminole!

Sweatlodge

Structure used for ritual purification by sweating from exposure to very hot fires or hot steam from pouring water over hot stones. Also called a sweathouse, for some tribes also doubling as clubhouses.

Stone-boiling

Cooking method by placing preheated stones into cooking vessels.

Sacred Bundles

A group of objects treasured by a tribe. They were well-guarded and often taken into battle. The items were publicly shown only on very important occasions.

Signals

Indian signs made with a pony, blanket, mirror, smoke, fire-arrow or other item to communicate over long distances.

Sequoya

This famous inventor of the Cherokee alphabet believed that writing and printing were very important to the white man, and would be so to the Indian. He was born around 1760 in the Cherokee town of Taskigi. His father was a white man; his mother was Cherokee. Growing up with the tribe, Sequoya was very creative at a young age. He liked to invent things, had a natural talent for mechanical workings and became an expert silversmith. A hunting accident crippled Sequoya for life. After the accident, he found a lot of time to study and think. Even though other kids teased him, he began to work on how his people could have a written alphabet like the white people did. He worked out a successful system of writing in the Cherokee language. In 1821, he presented his alphabet to the leaders of the Cherokee Nation, who approved it. In just a short time, many tribe members learned to read and write in their own language. The giant California redwood — Sequoia — is named for him.

Sachem

The supreme Indian ruler of an area where there are many related tribes.

23

Tobacco

A sacred plant early Indians used to make offering to their gods, cure diseases, bring good luck, seal agreements and bind treaties.

Tolemato

Yamasee village located on the coast around 1595. The Indians here revolted against the missionaries and drove them away for many years.

Tracking

To follow a trail by finding a sign such as a broken blade of grass, a moved stone or moccasin track. Indians learned to trail as children, so that they could find food, track enemies and disguise their own signs.

Treaties

Written agreements between the U.S. government and the Indians, most of which involved the Indians giving up their native lands.

Tomahawk

A club, axe or hammer used to chop wood, drive stakes in the ground or as a weapon.

Trail of Tears

After gold was discovered in Georgia, the white man was determined to force the Cherokee off their native lands. First the state began to claim such lands as their own. Some whites destroyed Cherokee farms and stole their horses and cattle. In 1838-39, the U. S. Army rounded up most of the Cherokee and marched them west in horrible weather. At least 1/4 of the Indians (4,000 of them!) died during this trip.

Tukpafka

Upper Creek village on Chattahoochee in 1777; name means "tinder" used for making fire.

Tuckaseegee

Cherokee village along Brasstown Creek near the Hiwassee River in Towns County.

Tomochichi

Old Indian warrior and chief of the Yamacraw. He welcomed the idea of English families settling peaceably with his people. For some reason he was outlawed by his own people. With a few followers, he settled where the city of Savannah is now located. He actually went to England with Gen. Oglethorpe, where he met King George II! While in England, he was given many presents and had his portrait painted. In 1899, a monument to him was erected in Savannah, where he had been given a public funeral.

Tribe

A group of Indians with shared culture, history, original territory, ancestry, social organization, and governmental structure. A tribe may contain several bands of Indians.

Thunderbird

A mythological Indian figure, as well as a part of the constellations for many Indians. Thunderbird mythology is mostly different from tribe to tribe, in general either coexisting with ancestors as an actual bird, or appearing as a spiritual nature god. The Thunderbird was good to the people in either case. Much mythology ties the thunderbird with thunder, lightning and storms.

24

Unique

The Yuchi, although part of the Creek Confederacy, were very different. They were tall, light-skinned and blue-eyed, and the women were noted for their beauty!

Unstoppable Wave

How could Georgia's Indian tribes cope with the onslaught of pioneers? They couldn't! From 1763-1773, the Creek and Cherokee were forced to surrender great tracts of land to the eager newcomers to Georgia, which was growing faster than any other English American colony.

U.S. Bureau of Indian Affairs

Provides public services such as law enforcement, land records, economic development, and education to Indians. Known for mismanagement and ethical problems.

U.S. Indian Schools

The Bureau of Indian Affairs operates hundreds of federal schools around the nation. Enrollment of Native American children measures in the thousands!

U.S. Indian Reorganization Act

Passed by Congress in 1934, the act authorized Indian tribes to establish and conduct their own governments, and to form businesses.

U.S. President

Once called Great White Father by Indians.

U.S. Colonists

Called Long Knives or Big Knives by early Indians, who also called English explorers "Coat Men."

U.S. Indian Wars

The U.S. War Department has compiled an official list of "Indian Wars" that occurred in the United States. Over 50 wars were fought between the U.S. and the Indians during the period of 1790-1850.

 **V** *is for . . .*

Vessels

Indians carried water in special gourds shaped liked bottles, called water vessels.

Village Councils

These were held in the town (council) house and occurred to discuss and decide important matters. Harmony and agreement was essential to tribal unity. Rather than vote on issues, they were discussed until everyone was satisfied. Anyone who wanted to could speak freely. Everyone did not always agree on the outcome, but everyone avoided conflict by pushing their case.

Vegetable Dyes

Indians could not buy color from the store like we can today. Instead, they created many different colors from the things they found on earth like plants, flowers, shrubs, trees, roots, and berries. They made beautiful and unique reds, oranges, yellows, greens, browns, and violets. These dyes were used for baskets, pottery, weaving, body makeup, and clothing.

Vann, Chief James

A leading citizen of the Cherokee. You can still see his Federal style brick home in the town of Spring Place. It was called the showplace of the Cherokee Nation when it was built in 1805.

Villages

Many Georgia Indians lived in villages! Villages were formed around different clans or bands within the tribe, but could also contain different clans living together. Villages were usually permanent settlements, although semi-nomadic tribes have been known to migrate between permanent villages.

Vesperic Indians

Indian tribes located in the United States.

W is for . . .

War Bonnet

Special headdress worn into battle, often adorned with feathers.

War Pony

Horse, often painted with colorful paint and ridden into battle.

What's in a Name?

The Savannah River and the city of Savannah are named for the Shawnee Indians! Their name meant "southerners." They were also called Savannah.

Wampum

Algonquian word for "white." This described beads or strings of beads made of clam or whelk shells. They were used in trade between the Indians and settlers. In 1640, counterfeit wampum was made! The Cherokee made wampum belts which showed the peace they had made with the Iroquois before the Revolutionary War. Some of these belts have been preserved by the Iroquois.

War Dance

Indian braves danced this before going into battle. The dance was a way of assembling the braves and getting them to commit to the fight ahead.

Well-Dressed Indians

Before you picture "Indians" running around in breechcloths, stop and picture the Seminole. The men were usually tall. They wore long, knee-length striped shirts that were tied at the waist by cords which had bags or pouches for pockets hanging from them. They also wore a turban decorated with plumes wound around the head!

Whistle

Indians from Georgia made them from the wing bones of birds. The whistles made the sound of the bird the bones came from! Used to communicate, signal, sound an alarm or even flirt with a maiden!

War Club

A weapon made of stone, bone, or wood in the shape of a club.

White Man

Indians generally called them Pale Face, a name the white men themselves suggested!

Women

Indian women in some tribes were poor and hardworking, like the men. But in some tribes, women had many rights, including becoming chief! In many southern tribes, women were chiefs. One example is the Lady of Cofitachiqui of Georgia.

27

Yamasee

Tribe that once lived on the Georgia and Florida coast. In 1570, the Spanish tried to take Indians who came to their missions to the West Indies to be slaves and the Yamasee revolted. In 1687, they went to South Carolina to live under English rule where they were treated poorly and fought against the English. Known for their canoe skills.

Yuchi

This tribe once lived in what is now Georgia. In 1966, an archaeologist discovered an ancient slab with symbols on it in the area of Georgia where the Yuchi once lived. Experts agree that this slab may have originated from the Mediterranean. This would mean that there was some form of communication or travel between the Old World and the New World about 3,000 years before Christopher Columbus!

Yazoo

As part of resolving the Yazoo Land Fraud in the state of Georgia, the Federal government promised in 1802 to remove the Cherokee Indians still living in the state. For 50 years, the Indians had tried to keep their homelands. But their stubbornness was no match for the white man's determination to settle on those very same lands.

▶▶▶ ZZZZZZ... ◀◀◀

Shamans and medicine men were not the only people who had access to the spirit world. Indians believed that people could make contact with spirits every night in their dreams! Dreamers could travel back to the time of man's creation or far ahead into their own futures. They also believed that dreams contained warnings or commands from the spirits. Many tribes felt that they had to act out their dreams as soon as they awoke. If an Indian dreamed about bathing, for example, he would run to his neighbors' houses first thing in the morning, and his neighbors would throw kettles full of cold water over him.

Yamacraw Indians

First met General James Oglethorpe when he sailed to Georgia to find a good place to settle the 35 English families he had with him.

Y... Or, "Why?"

1. Why do you think Indian warriors carried charms with them? Some Indian medicines have been scientifically proven to have true healing power and are still used today. Do you think their charms had any real power to help them win battles?
2. Why do you think the American government kept relocating Indians onto reservations and then making the reservations smaller and smaller?
3. Why did Indians use items such as a pipe in ceremonies? What kinds of symbolic objects do we use in ceremonies today?
4. Why and how did Indians use natural materials in creative ways?
5. Many Indian tribes are running successful businesses on their reservations today. There is one industry that many tribes are making a lot of money at. Do you know what this is? Hint: "I'll bet you do!"

28

Which Famous Native American Am I?

Solve the puzzle!

Down

1. This Shoshone woman joined Lewis and Clark as their guide and translator and helped make the expedition a success! Hint: She has 4 "a"s in her name!

4. This man gave the Cherokee their first alphabet so that they could write. Until then, they communicated only by speaking and drawing pictures. Hint: A famous ancient tree also has the same name!

5. He was one of the fiercest of Indian warriors! He fought against white settlers in Arizona and New Mexico to keep his people from being pushed off their lands. Hint: Jump!

Word Bank

| Black Elk | Crazy Horse | Sitting Bull | Sequoia |
| Sacajawea | Chief Joseph | Geronimo | Pocahontas |

Across

2. A legend says that this brave Algonquian woman saved the life of Englishman John Smith. Hint: Disney produced a movie about her.

3. He fought at Little Bighorn when he was only 13! He was also a wise "shaman" who saw visions and could advise people. Hint: Part of his name is an animal with antlers!

6. He was a great Sioux warrior who won the battle against General Custer at Little Bighorn in 1876. Hint: His horse was not crazy!

7. A leader of the Lakota (Sioux) tribe who lived on the Standing Rock Reservation in North Dakota after the battle of Little Bighorn. He tried to make conditions better for his people there, so the U.S. government called him a "troublemaker." Hint: He did not sit all the time!

8. A wise and brave chief of the Nez Percé who tried to bring his people to Canada to escape war. He said, "From where the sun now stands, I will fight no more forever." Hint: His father's name was "Old Joseph."

Different Ways for Different Indians!

North American Indian tribes are divided into different areas. In each of these areas, tribes shared common ways of living with each other. They might make similar arts or crafts, they might eat the same foods, or they might have had the same beliefs. These activities are all part of their "culture." Each area had its own culture, which was different from the tribes in all the other areas.

Below is a map of all the different groups of Indian tribes in North America. Color each area with a different color. You will see a colorful picture of how Native Americans can all be called "Indians" but still have very different cultures!

Celebration!

Powwows are big festivals where Native Americans gather to sing, dance, and eat together. It is a time to celebrate and show pride in their culture. Powwows can last from one afternoon to several days. The Indians dress in native costumes and dance ancient dances to the beating of drums.

Artists sell their arts and crafts. You might be able to buy some real Native American food cooked on an open fire. Native Americans go to powwows to be with each other, share ideas, and just have fun! Most powwows are also open to people who are not Indian. It's a great place to learn about Native American culture!

If you went to a powwow this weekend, what do you think you would see? What do you think might NOT be there? Circle the objects you think you would see at a powwow. Put an X through those you probably won't see.

Answer Key: Circled objects are: beads, moccasins, open fire, drums, feathers, baskets, kids, food, drums, horse.

Make an Indian Weaving!

Many Native Americans used weaving to create useful things like sashes (belts), bags, mats, and blankets. They used animal hair to make yarn, and dyed the yarn with natural dyes from fruits and other plants. They also used some plant fibers, like cotton, to make weaving thread.

Weave a small Native American mat of your own. Use different colors of yarn to create a beautiful pattern in your weaving. Place a favorite object on the mat or hang it on your wall!

Prepare the "loom"
Cut a piece of cardboard 5 inches wide and 6 inches long. Along the two 5-inch sides (the "short" sides), have an adult cut slits 1/4 inch deep. These slits should be 1/2 inch apart from each other. So, on each short side you will have 9 slits.

Directions:
1. Take a long piece of yarn and bring it from the back through the first slit (the one next to the edge of the cardboard.) The end of the yarn will hang down behind the cardboard.

2. Bring the yarn right across the front of the cardboard to the slit opposite the one your yarn came through.

3. Now bring the yarn under the back of the cardboard and then up again through the second slit.

4. Repeat #2 and #3, until you have 9 strands of yarn across the front of your cardboard!

5. Then cut the yarn and tie the two loose ends in the back of the cardboard.

6. Take another piece of yarn and start feeding it through the 9 strands, going over one, under the next over the next, etc. When you get to the end, pull the yarn behind the cardboard and around to the front, and begin again. This time, whatever strand you went over, go under. And whatever strand you went under, go over.

7. Repeat this pattern until the front of your cardboard in covered. Then cut the yarn in the back of the cardboard, and trim it to create a fringe for your mat!

Tips:
• For a wild look, use variegated or different colored yarn!
• For a tighter mat, push the under/over strands up against the previous strands during weaving.
• To keep your mat from unravelling, tie neighboring fringe together up close to the mat.

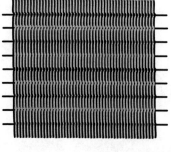

32

Finders Keepers?

Native Americans have many buried treasures. For hundreds of years, special objects would sometimes be buried with Native Americans, or maybe they would just be lost. Archeologists used to dig for interesting artifacts in old Native American gravesites. They would keep the Native American bones or the arrowheads, rattles, masks and other objects that they found. But this made the Native Americans feel like they were being robbed.

In 1990, the U.S. government passed a law that said that no one could look for or take these Native American objects anymore. And whoever had any already had to give them back to the people they belonged to. This is called repatriation

Help the archeologist return the artifact to a Native American.

FINISH

START

Fast Fact

An artifact is an object that was made by people a long time ago for some useful purpose.

33

Busy Hands!

Before modern times, Native Americans didn't have stores where they went to buy things. They made everything they needed.

What did Indians make with their own hands? Use the Word Bank and pictures to find out!

Word Bank

blanket	moccasins	arrows	pottery	canoe
mat	food	jewelry	pouch	box

_ _ _ _ _ _ _ _   _ _ _ _ _ _ _

_ _ _ _ _ _ _   _ _ _ _ _ _ _

_ _ _ _ _ _ _ _ _

_ _ _ _ _ _ _

_ _ _ _ _ _ _ _ _ _

_ _ _ _ _ _ _ _ _

_ _ _ _ _ _ _ _ _

_ _ _ _ _ _ _ _ _ _ _

American Indians Today

Beginning with the first letter of each group of letters, cross out every other letter to discover some new words. You may not have heard of these before, but you can read all about them!

1. Many Indians live on these, but many more do not!

TRYELSDEBRNVJAOTPIPOWNASX

_____

2. Many Indians have been poor for a long time because for many years the government took away their lands and their ability to make a living.

TPKOOVWEBRNTXYA

_____

3. Many Indians have been studying hard at school and going to college in order to earn more money. Education helps the Indians make their lives better. These Native Americans are working to become:

TSJUMCBCFEYSMSOFPUVL

_____

4. This is a big term that means Native Americans have worked hard to get the U.S. government to let them rule themselves. This means that they have their own laws and make their own decisions. They are like a separate country inside the U.S.! Now, try and see if you can get your parents to give you the same thing!

TSGENLBF   **JDGEETSEWRAMCIHNUAKTYIKOTNU**

_____

Fast Fact

What do Indians work as today?

- doctors
- nurses
- factory workers
- artists
- lawyers
- actors

The same kinds of jobs any American might work at!

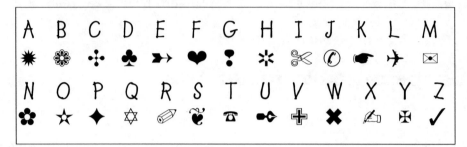

Native Americans Move to the City!

Solve the code to discover the mystery words!

A	B	C	D	E	F	G	H	I	J	K	L	M
N	O	P	Q	R	S	T	U	V	W	X	Y	Z

1. During the 1950s and 1960s, the American government paid Indians to leave their homes on reservations and move to cities to get jobs. If cities are sometimes called urban areas, then these brave Indians were called:

_____ _____ _____ _____ _____   _____ _____ _____ _____ _____ _____ _____

2. Many Indians chose to stay on their reservations and not move to the city. They thought that if they moved to the city, they would lose the way of life that their parents and ancestors had taught. These Indians called themselves:

3. Native Americans who moved to cities lived close to each other. They tried to keep their way of life as much as possible. They did not want to forget their religion, native art, or music. They did not want to lose their:

4. Are you afraid of heights? Many people are. The Mohawk Indians are not! Many of them work hundreds of feet above the city to build steel frames for skyscrapers. People who do this work above the city are:

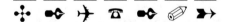

5. Today urban Indians and reservation Indians come together to celebrate their culture. They share ideas and stories. They dance and beat drums. They make and sell Indian jewelry. During these celebrations, Indians remember how much they have to be proud of! These big parties are called